Would-Land

Would-Land

Jill Alexander Essbaum

Cooper
Dillon

Would-Land
Copyright © 2020 by Jill Alexander Essbaum
All rights reserved. First edition.

Cooper Dillon Books
San Diego, California
CooperDillon.com

Cover Design & Interior by Adam Deutsch

ISBN-13: 978-1943899-10-4

CONTENTS

OH WANDERER	1
SHE WAS DRIVEN BY A THOUSAND DESIRES, A FEW OF THEM DECENT	3
APOLOGIA	4
THE RUN-DOWN	6
DOOR	7
PASSAGE	8
IN THE HARD DARK	9
ZÜRICH HAUPTBAHNHOF	10
NON REDIBIMUS	11
LET ME TELL YOU	12
STAYS	15
THE HOURS	16
RAPSFELD	17
EASTER	18
I DREAMED	20
SOME OTHER'S DAY	21
EVERYWHERE A MAGPIE	23
YOU CANNOT RESCUE A WOMAN FROM HERSELF	24
4:13 A.M.	25
OUTSIDE	26
CHANGE OF ADDRESS	27
WHAT ISN'T MINE	28
POEM	31
SHE SPENT A YEAR HALLUCINATING BIRDS	32
A SUITCASE	33
EQUIVOCATIONS	34
GREIFENSEE	35
A ROSE IS A ROSE IS A ROSE IS A ROSE IS	37
MISERERE MEI	38
WHAT A DREAM I HAD	40
HELL	41
TWO STORY	42
IM FRIEDHOF	44

HELL IS OTHER PERSON	45
ILLUSION	46
TO VANISH	47
CIVIL TWILIGHT	49
I AM MOST MYSELF	50
PARTING SONG	51
NEIN	52
EPISTOLARY	53
INSOMNIA IS LONELY	56
TIME	57
TEAR	58
PRECIPICE	59
YES, BAUM	61
NIGHTWALK	65
THE WISTFUL	66
WOULD-LAND	68
MARGINALIA	71
ZÜRICHHORN	80
ACKNOWLEDGMENTS AND NOTES	82

OH WANDERER

You rise pre-dawn before it dawns upon
                the roses to grow open, and you go

in South's direction through a city
                that's proclaimed you its strangest

of strangers. It's May. You march
                with a springheel danger like a dagger-

handed man who is his own arch foe.
                These streets? You do not know them.

But you do. Every step seems stopgap.
                That bus bench. These bike racks.

On your back, a frayed, gray sweater,
                old with holes. In your pack, those dozen

brick-red dreads you've picked to pitch
                at windows. It is the best bad idea

you've had in months. But your targets
                are in hiding. Your bull's eye is a secret.

You're aiming at ghosts in snow. It's May.
                Pre-dawn. You pace these paths alone,

placing each step as if it were a wager
                that there'll never be another. You bypass

a rank of apartments, press past
                a parking lot, locked at the gate. A mile away

there's fields of rape, the stammer
>	of a pending train, and rainclouds shifting

in the tensile dark. It's May. You might.
>	You try to be a wife. You try to be

mundane. The fog is not your friend
>	and dawn is nowhere to be found.

Don't be so certain what you are is sad.
>	You circle the fountain in the square,

reflect on your reflection in the storefront
>	of the hair salon. The auto repair.

The fix-it shop. Then, you move along.
>	They are all wrong streets.

>	>	You take each one.

SHE WAS DRIVEN BY A THOUSAND DESIRES, A FEW OF THEM DECENT

She was easier done than said.
She was oftener sad than sunny.
If she dealt a round of rummy,
It was simply for the gin.
And she let everyone win.

And she led everybody on.
She was on every body like hide on a hog.
Her climate a hybrid of chaos and fog.
She measured her weathers in knots and lunar spools.
And whether or not you wooed her,

She'd swoon. She mooned for the scrub
Of many tongues and manly tamps.
Lovers with archer's arms and matador hands.
(She landed doormats and saps.)
She meant no harm. She hummed no tune.

But O, what blues she succumbed to.
And O, those fools she would run to.
Hers, a strong will, but a very weak won't.
A cog in the wheel of every damn want.
And wherever she went she got caught,

Caught cold. She grew old, old, old.
And she groaned. And she grinded.
(Nobody minded.) The bone
Of her heart never mended its break.
Her boat sprung a leak in the lake of *Too Late*.

She chased what she craved. It left her winded.
Her grave was left untended.

APOLOGIA

> *However innocent your life may have been, no Christian ought to venture to die in any other state than that of the penitent.* —St. Augustine

I have been sodden with wine.
I have been confused by wine.
I have been lied to by men,
And yet, I lie down upon such men,
Still and willing in the manners that they please.
Lord, I've been the blemish at your love feast.

And I've been tangled in nettles and brambles,
Have dwelt in seamy hotels, have ambled
Down roads that once, so necessary,
Seemed. And I've prayed, hot and overloadedly.
Having meddled in such matters
That ought be closed to me.

Darkness, I have done dread deeds in,
Hearkening to apocalyptic heathen,
Even as I cocked my lips to yours. And I have slept
On floors. And I have crept along on all fours.
And. More. I have lived briskly in nice houses.
I have swigged whiskey in icehouses.

I have been June, July, and August.
I have been riotous when I felt like I must
Or I could be. And I've hung on your tree like a ripe fig
Desiring to be plucked. And I've flung my body to your bed
Like a white bride pining to be rubbed up against.
Like a suckling child hungry in a viper's den.

And I have been Dismas, the penitent
Thief. And I have been Judas. And I've spent
My plenty silvers chiefly on my hells.
In that, I have seldom, if ever, failed.
It's just as well. For as the ibis devours her carrion,
I feed upon what queasy defeats I carry on

My back. Thus the beggar becomes her bowl.
And the hangwoman surrenders to the scaffold.
And irrevocable acts of god and doom consume me.
Can this be mercy? I fear there isn't any
Left. Even the chrism is bereft.
Wretched, most wretched it says,

While my guilt unfolds like a napkin in your lap.
Will a dog grow fat on crumbs the Master drops?
I have been a grabber at your garment hem.
And I have been a Magdalene outside your tomb.
And I've bathed atop roofs, have pounded with rue,
Have pooled my pearls, the sorrowful few—

Like milky mea culpas they rattle fragile on a string.
Christ: Forgive me *everything*.

THE RUN-DOWN

Cold, but she never wore overcoats.
Tired, but her cot was rotten and worn.
At a quarter to ten she tried every door.

She had two dry eyes and a mute, mocking pout,
And six dire doubts and seventeen heavens,
And a God who wouldn't commute her sentence.

She was taxed in a bracket and tossed in a bucket.
She cheated on husbands and sought out her exes.
They didn't quite hate her so they didn't quite hit her.

She sloshed through mornings with tonic and vodka.
And her coughs were chronic, her symbols iconic,
She rationed her reason in droppers and thimbles.

She wept when she walked and the law tried to bust her.
The library shushed her and slapped her with fines.
Her fingernails spiked like tines on a fork.

So she sated her sorrows in sewers and brothels
And itched for the answers her brothers denied her.
She throbbed like a wound that swallowed its knife.

And her butters were margarine, her jewels were paste.
The worse the poison, the sweeter the taste.

DOOR

Half wall, half hole, part port. A kind of gate. But wait—it's not. Locked in? You're out of luck. Don't knock it till you've tried it. Someone might be sleeping. A peek thru the key-slot's as good as a bell-ring. For a knob's a thing of beauty. Brass apple. Shiny knurl. Hold it. Spin it. Wait for the click. Shoulder it open. Go in.

PASSAGE

At mourning, I'm a laureate.
Cast this head on a brass coin.
I'll assume a glass crown.

This morning, I wake to inner alarm.
The guess that darkness isn't all
there is. That there is more,

that the relative next is worse.
Sunrise is glacial. The snow
is chalk. I lilt when I walk,

like a drunk. A reproach of birds
condemns me. Am I game? Don't
shoot. I pitch from one periphery

to its brother. I am a chill
that can't be burned away. Not
with sunlight, not with love.

Of course there is something
worse to come. Like: when god
doesn't answer my prayer. Like:

when god does.

IN THE HARD DARK

When you are alone.
When even the ghost is gone.
When the erring end of night
knots itself into a stopper.
When the clock's locked in
and the telephone moans.
When what's wrong is what
you long for, and it shows
itself in shadows. And when
the shadows worsen. When
they swerve and persevere.
When the pitch is raw and
warbled and perverse. When
it speeds and when it slows
like a runner who can't pace.
When a serpent gives chase
and the snake is real. When
it cracks through your pavement
and makes you surreal.
The dead are always dead.
They never say a word.
In the hard dark the heart holds
the hurt.

ZÜRICH HAUPTBAHNHOF

Every bench-bank is a waiting room.
And every clock's a plot to tick me off.
A seller vends cut tulips from a booth.
A tourist asks the way to Lindenhof.

A luggage cart requires a two-franc piece.
I cannot be too frank. I am a wreck.
A young Swiss Army soldier bends his knees
And rifles for a lighter in his pack.

This was a hub. It's now a terminus.
A woman's voice announces S-Bahn trains.
The bus bay and the taxi ranks don't budge.
I whip around, convinced I've heard my name.

A common robin pecks a Brötli crust.
On platform fifty-three I miss you most.

NON REDIBIMUS

We shall not come again, not to this wet
                and summer day, nor to the waylaid place

where you laid waste to me and I to you,
                and where we reminisced recalling who

did what to whom. We shall not come again.
                Not to the bed we thrashed nor to the memory

of the way I brushed my hair back, nights,
                nor to the air we dared to share to breathe,

or couldn't quite. We shall not come again.
                No more, my face seen round your corner, or

your briefcase found beneath my table. We
                weren't able, apt or sane. We shall not come

again. Nor cry nor clutch, not even once
                again. We shall not cover up in quilts

or bear the beast of one another's guilts
                or sit in silences made saddest by

                what was. We shall not come again. *Because.*

LET ME TELL YOU

what it's like to get left
on a jetty in a tatty,

wet dress that doesn't
fit and never did;

or how summer's
spleen stood ground

that day at the docks
when swans

and gulls flew
up and the sea-sick

girl notched a mark
on her arm,

kicked out into
an inlet, then failed to

run ashore; or how the bay
at daybreak

pools up bullet blue;
or why rubies are most beautiful

when rubbed; and what
it feels like when a coast

goes clear; or how
to be nowhere

that anyone knows of, or no
one any body knows;

and who's on waterfront
foot patrol; and who he's looking

out for; and why it's always
ladies doing lighthouse keeping

here; and how damp lamps can
brighten heavy homes; and

that once I was a lover
of both rivers and revolvers;

and that if you are a boat
then I am a tree

on the periphery of pain;
and that this is not a wave

it is a black, brick wall
that shears through water

like a saw through a tree
on the periphery

of pain; and how old ropes
and thin-boned moments

snap in half; and how
we are just two

more storms *(I harbor no*
ill will); and that ferries do

exist but I don't
take them—*seriously*—they sink;

and how the noose
has looped

its knot
because

the tie has turned;
and why the ocean burns.

STAYS

Everything alludes to the mood of us.
This color, for instance, the color of you.
Blood-blue like the walls of the house we share.
Blue-black like the ravels in my hair.

Everything habituates the shatter of our glass.
This tiger of yours that mauls on command.
Or yours, the upper hand of dispute.
The furnace you promised to fix but *good*—

But didn't. But haven't. Or: *Won't. Ain't gonna.*
A tainted summer of untoward words.
The unnerved synapse twixt *said* and *heard*.
The lapse in my verve,

The slap of your verbs.
How every well we've dowsed runs dry.
The drowsy *oh wells,* the soused betrothals,
The stab-wounds we dressed up in bedclothes.

Everything augments the flaw of us.
The lusters we lack, the lusts we've glutted,
The delusions we've slutted on analyst's couches.
Your Stalinist urges. My purges. I reach

For the one-two punch of panic pills.
You sit and sort the bills. *A pair of parallel hells.*
The gods that goad us know our names.
The books you read disclaim my pain—

And everything stays the same, the same.

THE HOURS

froze then thawed.
They came to a roil,
then settled on a simmer,
then served up summer
on a stove plate
to a pair of lover's palates
while the timer ticked through
everything they wished.

Then it was Thursday.
Then it was the middle
of the month. And then
the something that wasn't
turned into a nothing
that was. September
was a stranger. A later
stage of leftover gone

rotten. Then forgotten.

RAPSFELD

Morning, I wake to that shuddering
        house and I'm urged to follow

a daylight moon. The sky's attuned.
        What's path is prologue. I'm passed

by a man and his dog. The man bears
        bare and rabid teeth. I respond

out of grief and habit alike. Graffiti
        mars a barn like a birthmark. A rued,

bidden tension clenches the wind.
        And I am in a field of rape again.

And sadness is meant to be had. And
        tears speak louder than terrors or

prayers. I do not trust this yellow field.
        Nor the feel of your face in my hands.

Nor the lug-around lump of love
        in my throat, its oilseed luster, its ill-

tempered smoke. So my backbite
        bites back on a slackjaw scar for

the vow I made to last night's stars,
        and the jaundiced terrain that used

        to be ours.

EASTER

is my season
of defeat.

Though all
is green

and death
is done,

I feel alone.
As if the stone

rolled off
from the head

of the tomb
is lodged

in the doorframe
of my room,

and everyone
I've ever loved

lives happily
just past

my able reach.
And each time

Jesus rises
I'm reminded

of this marble
fact:

they are not
coming back.

I DREAMED

That I hacked you into pieces.
Then fed you to my animals,

the pigs, the lambs, the geese.
And then I took them to the fair,

where a butcher bought the lot.
I didn't look back when he loaded

them up. And then, with my profit,
I bargained a dress. Its buttons

were beaks. Its silk, spun of sows'
ears. It was blue and it bleated

and it seeped when I walked. I
wore it to church. I wore it to bed.

I wore it to the inquest when
they quizzed me on your death.

I didn't do anything wrong!, I said,
and the stubble-chinned judge agreed. But

when I woke there was blood
on the sheets.

SOME OTHER'S DAY

Sunday and the sky I long for
is a hateful gray shade that I
have never seen up close,
with undertones of elephants
in dust storms, running from
the tusk hunter's gun. But no.
All clouds are gone. I can't
be bothered with breakfast.
Instead I chew down bones
from yesterday's lost argument,
when a bubble of blood
misunderstood my intent.
Two months, we roomed in
like newlyweds, slept in one
bed, ran tandem errands,
tittered over nonesuch *this*es
and *that*s and made lunch
of the world's most foolish foods.
And it was good.

Today the sunshine sings
and I hate it. Ladies at church
pin blooms to their breasts
but mum's the word on me.
Some subjects can't be broached.
So I sit alone and take notes
on issues I know nothing about
in the margin of a bible my own
mother bought.

Though Jesus walked free
from the deadman's womb,
I have nowhere to go but home
where the yard's breezy trees
indifference me in a manner

antiseptic and black. For even
they accept the fact that sometimes
an acorn will grow up to be an oak.
And sometimes it won't.

EVERYWHERE A MAGPIE

One for sorrow, two for mirth, three for a wedding, four for death.
—traditional country proverb

the magpie he kept unslept for five or six years
the magpie who circled the ruin of his stone-cobbled square
the magpie who squared his circles without any compass
the magpie whose whiplash tongue he never grew tired of
the magpie alit on the roof of his second wife's cottage
the magpie who soared in a sky pricked sore by spires
the magpie so fond of all shine that she clung to his switchblade
the magpie he sloughed like a snake's winter skin in the springtime
the magpie pragmatic who kept her own name on the house note
the magpie who fashioned their nest out of paper and birch bark
the magpie who leapt to her death from an interstate overpass
the magpie he dressed in furs from his great aunt's travel trunk
the magpie whose silks got caught in the spokes of his tires
the magpie who, bored of his sulking, went out with the raven
the magpie who, toying his rifle, went out with a bang
the magpie who swooped when she ought to have perched on her swing
the magpie who slept at the foot of his fold-out sofa bed
the magpie who bled and bled and bled and bled

YOU CANNOT RESCUE A WOMAN FROM HERSELF

Born a sinner, she got so much better at it as she went along. She groaned upon grindstones. She studied certain birdsongs. She was nothing but bone and episodic sorrow. Was she pretty? Pretty got her into trouble. There were gashes in her satchel. Her eyes were deniable. Her flaw was fundamental. What canny, shrewd words she wondered aloud! Her knees were sore and she fretted over God. She trod through miles of agony, simpering. Hers were the sins of submitting. Hers were petty treasons done precisely to her liking. Like the Viking for whom no Iceland sufficed. Like civil twilight settling in the sky. When she went away she did not say why. She mopped up the poppies. She undermined the clouds. She stood out in crowds. She cleaned up rooms. She chased men into underglooms. Black hyacinth grew in her garden. She handled hard-ons. She begged no pardon. She loved most who did not love her back. Unflappable woman, she flapped. Like an accident she happened. She shunned the vast passive. Her losses, her lips. She scryed a crystal ball of absolute error. She catalogued each terror. It wasn't fair. She did not go far. She died among strangers. She zigged and then she zaggered. Her knack was in her hammering. There was misery in her rubric. Her stigmata was invisible. She ate the poisoned apples. She grappled with an angel. The answer she sought wasn't found in the mail. She went to jail. She went to hell. She wore every want like a shawl. She shook like a dice cup. She slept on her stomach. She strummed her own blossom. She lusted on hoodlums, changed colors in the autumn. Once, and out of boredom, she got very drunk. Then jumped.

4:13 A.M.

The shift of sleepwalks and suicides.
The occasion of owls and a demi-lune fog.
Even God has nodded off

And won't be taking prayers til ten.
Ad interim, you put them on.
As if your wants could keep you warm.

As if. You say your shibboleths.
You thumb your beads. You scry the glass.
Night creeps to its precipice

And the broken rim of reason breaks
Again. An obsidian sky betrays you.
Every serrate shadow flays you.

Soon enough, the crow will caw.
The cock will crow. The door will close.
(He isn't coming back, you know.)

And so wee, wet hours of grief relent.
In thirty years you might forget
Precisely how tonight's pain felt.

And in whose black house you dwelt.

OUTSIDE

A worsening snow. And a sense that someone's coming. (Or, no?) Losing is an orgy of the solipsistic sort. You fuck yourself over. And over again. And every woe you've ever known joins in. Outside, a thousand apple trees are growing, growing, gone. (Or maybe only one?) Last year I clambered branches just to peek from the perch where waxwings sing. I saw a house, a town, a street. There was a farm. There was a park. A child's swing keened in an apoplectic breeze. Outside, the wind's an imp. A trickster who spins jokes at my expense. In winter nobody wins. The driveway is a ring, a rink. Your car's gone missing again. You hate me in a glacial way. Over eras and in sheets. The air affixes sleet to sky. I stand in the center of my blizzard. I wait for a sign.

CHANGE OF ADDRESS

After
the Mister

dis-missed
his Missus,

she dwelt
in a private

apart-
ment.

WHAT ISN'T MINE

Let us tunnel
through the rubble,

through the thrum.
Let us rut through the sum

of who we were,
or are,

or will be in the years to come:
a couple

of someones
who used to be in love.

Used to be in love.
Ho. Hum.

These days: *Seem to be in hate.*
Gypsum, marble, pyrite, slate.

See here? A pit of snakes.
Look there. The rock of your rages.

And I'm in a cable-cage, slinking down your shaft.
You fondle that hefty *What if...?* as if

to hurl it. All the other holes
are blatant hells.

A dragline scrapes our fossicked floor.
I am the ether. You are the ore.

This is the war that nobody won.
Like afterdamp collapsing a lung.

You take to swinging a pick-axe.
I take back my vamping kinks

And the pavement beneath us sinks.
This stinks. Think: *In-situ leaching*

but with leeches, louses,
lampreys. Oh Spouse,

your hard hat leaks a surfeit
of lamp rays that's wasted sub-surface.

A night so pitch it's perfectly black.
A sapphire scarred by a scratch.

Sickness, health, abundance, lack.
The salt in my wound. The shirt off your back.

So our bloodcup runs empty of urge.
The metallurgy

we're made of demands its dirge.
Our burrows diverge.

Our passages split.
Copper, silver, gravel, grit.

Am I—perhaps—alluvial?
Un-live-with-able?

A bit too simple or silty?
Only gold ought be gilty.

And you are as cold as coal.
I am your dole, your lode,

your carbon-flawed diamond.
All told: We drilled and hit demons.

Granite, though, is good for graves.
Granted, a mine isn't quite a cave.

What isn't mine, I cannot give.

POEM

A Clementine
Of inclement climate
Grows tart.

A crocus
Too stoic to open,
Won't.

Like an oyster
That cloisters a spoil of pearls,
Untouched—

The heart that's had
Enough
Stays shut.

SHE SPENT A YEAR HALLUCINATING BIRDS

They perched on roofs and fences and sills. They posed statue-still on catenary lines. They aligned along cables like prayer beads on rope. They amassed en masse on the cemetery lawn and marauded the broad, yawning fields like cattle. Their cackles were black. Each shadow dove and pecked. They nested in chimneys and chirped at the chime of the church bell. They worked in shifts. Clocked out at odd hours. They laid their eggs in the Vs of trees. They teemed on the dry-baked banks of creeks, streams the sun had overseen. They teetered on the bed-knob tops of flagpoles. They pitched like pennies into founts or babies into wells. They paced her train and lunged the platform when she disembarked. They thumped her doors then skulked away like hoodlum teens. They jabbed her. When she cried they did it faster. Everyone knows what happened next. They grew in size. They multiplied in sum. Some as big as sunflower stalks. Others tall like bonfire flames. Or moving vans. Or the sick, brick houses people die inside of every night. Their hatchlings canopied the sky. Was it her fault, then, when they pinned her to the ground and thrust their feathers down her throat? Or wormed between her legs in bad-man ways? Or rattled plumes and whooped and beat her body with their wings? Or locked their talons to her thighs and *tra-la-la*-ed that ditty from the old-time music box? They forced their whiskies past her lips and put her in the pillory. This was foreplay, in a way. They rolled in rabid packs and woofed like dogs. She couldn't throw a bone. The meat was gone. They chased her and they named her and they boiled her tears and bathed her. Then they ate her.

A SUITCASE

isn't suited for suits, truth told.
Most useful when holding

what's easy to fold, pants for example,
or anything slack. A jacket,

like breasts in a too-tight dress,
won't fit unless

jammed in. All spills out.
We cram it back. But

rumpled twill will never flatter
anyone and blazers

take ages to iron. How depressing,
then, that dead-weight

haversack, some saddlebag
I'm saddled with, the sadness

I packed like a school-trip sack
lunch. Everyone's got baggage.

Each of us, a case in point.
Like you. A coat

that's woven of *gold* and *gone*.
I've nothing left to carry on.

EQUIVOCATIONS

The map is not the landscape.
The recipe isn't the dinner.
The polygraph isn't the falsehood.
The confession isn't the sinner.

The diagram isn't the sentence.
The blueprint isn't the house.
The jacket blurb isn't the novel.
The groom is not the spouse.

The outline isn't the essay.
The evidence isn't the crime.
The seismogram isn't the earthquake.
The tears are not the crying.

GREIFENSEE

Let's say you are a man whose summer suit is white.
        You're on a stroll around a lake in mid-July
when a woman on a bicycle rides past you.
        She's small and pale as lace, transparent in a way
that makes you wonder whether she's a ghost. But let's
        say that she's not. And let's say when she passes you
she turns around to wink or pedals slower, maybe
        stops. And let's say that she's young. And that her face
has claimed your memory and in that moment you
        forget whatever it was you thought you knew about
a woman at all. What she wants. Where she hides
        her promises and how an empty room might be
her enemy. It's after afternoon and soon
        the sun will set upon the matte-black lake. And you
will fall in love before moonrise, impossible though
        it sounds. And you will hide among her willows. She
will call you Soldierman because you're absolutely
        brave. *A brick box begs to be unlocked and you're
the key*, she'll say, and even the ring-necked duck will blush.
        Her sentences are prayers. The day proves providential.
You thank God.

        Now. Let's say none of this is true. It's not a summer
suit you wear but a thick, wool jacket zipped to your chin.
        There is no man. No bicycle. And you're the only
woman in this scene. You move by power of broken
        leg (a metaphor, but *still*). And mid-July
is really early March. And it's damn cold. The air
        is gray, opaque with rain and terrible, practical hate.
And you are vague and pale as lace. The coins you toss
        have no coincidence. And you've forgotten what
you want. And every empty room's your enemy
        and everything's an empty room. It's almost noon

and soon the bells of the old, stone church will ring and ring.
      And you're old too. You do not stop or slow or turn
around. There are no willows. You're alone. A brick
      box beckons you inside of it. Nothing of you
isn't ghost. You've fallen. But it's not in love.
      And the problem with Hell is that it's eternal.
The lake is matte black. There are no prayers. There is
      no God. A fog comes in. When it rolls out, the birds
are gone.

A ROSE IS A ROSE IS A ROSE IS A ROSE IS

a woman who supposes
that a flower feels remorse
but knows, of course, that thorns
will only mourn the thumbs
they do not prick, and how
even the comeliest petal
can't settle a score, a bar tab,
a bet, and that what is scent
isn't always saved, and a rose,
like love, will decay.

MISERERE MEI

Four decades
I've hoped for
a scruple of proof
to sustain my longest
longed-for truth—
that my limbic brain
isn't just some drop
and swindle shyster
swapping bundles
of probable greenbacks
for genuine lack, and
that somehow the ache
of my start-stop faith
determines that I am—
in some way—OK.
That God is God, and I,
if not exactly ironclad
good, am enough of a kind
of kindness to suffice
as nice. But that is not
the case.

My days are wet
and same. I wake
to pervious letdowns.
The entitlements
of coffee. The spleen
of a torn tea towel,
neurotic, if not neutral.
The phone call I regret,
the one I've not yet
placed. The iterate,
scapegrace prayer
that never veers:

God?—be there. But
kitchen petitions usually
land in the scrap bin.
With the peels
and the rinds and
the skins. For the end
of one thing isn't
always the beginning
of another.

At two a.m. the sky
is patent black and
I stand at the center
of all my mistakes.
It's winter. I am naked.
I may not be awake.
The air is vaguely
prussic, and all the bees
have left. And sleep
is the youngest brother
of death. Christ, I am
so empty that I've broken
apart a heart I didn't
even know I owned,
a second one holed up
in the ship-hold of the first
like an immigrant
indentured to a servitude
of tears. At two a.m.
the imminent rockrose
nears. I plead my mercies

here.

WHAT A DREAM I HAD

and you were in it.
First we made the bed,
and then we stripped it.
And then, we strapped
each other to ourselves
and did rough things
while wrapped in cream-
pink linens. Ghost, we
played, beneath the sheets.
I lost each *mother-may-I*
game. You cried when
you came and I laughed,
laughed, laughed at
the certainty of our dirty
curtains. But the blighted,
white sentry of sleep
(as is custom) grew bored
at sun-up, then left
its post. And when I woke
I was alone. And
the morning did nobody
justice. And the room
felt like a room I knew,
but it was under water.
And I was a kind of fire
you couldn't put out.
The aftermath of sex
is always doubt.

HELL

Hot as.
Road to.
Give me.
Shot to.
Fight like.
Put through.
What the.
Go to.

TWO STORY

They lock the door and then repair
to sovereign floors of the house they share
split by a flight of stairs.

In the kitchen, a kettle airs its grievance
with a know-nothing wheeze
as he steeps a green tea blackly.

The agony, it's called, when leaves unclench
like fists post-punch. He can't recall
when last they kissed. Or touched.

Above, she drubs the windowpane
again and again and again and again
as if to weaponize her doom.

A mood bleeds through the room
like oil through gauze.
But every story has two sighs,

and nine wrecked hours of night
remain to reckon. She sleeps
in the attic because it beckons.

He paces the basement, blue
as a fuse. Resistor or breaker—
no matter—the aftermaths match.

And his room's roof is her
foundation. A margin splits
the situation. Steps are taken

but none are brought back.
The edifice lists on an axis of lack.
They peer at each other with spiraling stares.

The fulcrum of their house is tiers.

IM FRIEDHOF

In your black coat I walk into June heat.
You take a dark bird's shape and fly away.
I see your ghost, but it does not see me.

The recently bereaved are hard to please.
I didn't make your bed or your mistakes.
In your black coat I walk into June heat.

A phantom bone that haunts its amputee,
Of all my specters, you are most awake.
I see your ghost, but it does not see me.

I pilfer through these memories like a thief.
But maybe all's not lost. Some's just misplaced.
In your black coat I walk into June heat

And I keen once more for your mortal hands beneath
What gravid fabrics other fingers braid.
I see your ghost, but it does not see me.

So I sail, half-masted, through the ghastly sea
Of these wasted, assailing lovers, loss and fate.
In your black coat I walked into June heat.
I did not leave your ghost. But it left me.

HELL IS OTHER PERSON

Not nearly as easy to drop you
As it was to pick you up.

Well, fuck.

ILLUSION

Disease preceded our union.
Then, you saw us in half.
Quel legerdemain, this vanishing act!
A single spell, a sleight of hell—
We're nothing? Up yours. Leave.
Voilà. The magic's gone.
So I move on.

TO VANISH

is to effervesce.
To tissue-thin

yourself, be
plasma-less.

To flip a switch.
Lay down upon

a pulpit. To go,
and then be mist.

To condense
yourself, Dear

Droplet, and
evaporate

like lake-fog
underneath

noon sun.
To pend from

a rope and get
it done with.

To slide through
fire in a hurt-

heart way. Be
burnt. Bit off.

Then swallowed
by the sky.

To die.

CIVIL TWILIGHT

What's left of the last light's been locked out.
        Like a bell-booked wraith that's blocked

from the chapel, it haunts each edge of this purlieu
        in exile, a plight that the sky won't resign to.

And dusk's hazel eye can't be trusted. What's
        near appears distant, while things remote are

fictive. Your kindness comes off as vindictive. And
        sunsets are always ill omens, for what isn't illumed

is unknown. When mourning stars are evening
        out, night arrives with a cataleptic halt. Baths,

then battle lines are drawn. I don my darkest
        shadow as the blue hour blackens, burns. And

        beg you to return.

I AM MOST MYSELF

When dispossessed.
When gone or impossible.
When I'm fraudulent
Or automaton-ish.

When almost a trauma.
When Christly. When cross.
When little lamb lostly.
When just because.

When I'm a pauper.
When I'm a laundress.
When first incautious,
Then applauded.

And when in August
I'm accosted.
When apostolic.
When exhausted.

When in peril.
When post-coital.
When I'm a ghost.
When I'm in hell.

When a grizzled laugh
Onslaughts.
When pissed up.
When fucked off.

And when in a black room
I'm attacked
By that stonework sadness
And I don't fight back.

PARTING SONG

First
it is one day without you.

Then two.
And soon

our point: *moot*.
And our solution, diluted.

And our class action (if ever was)
is no longer suited.

Wherewith I give to looting through
the war chest of our past

like a wily Anne Bonny
who snatches at plunder or graft.

But the wreck of that ransack,
that strongbox, our splintering coffer,

the claptrap bastard
of the best we had to offer,

is sog-soaked and clammy,
empty but for sand.

Like the knuckle-white cup
of my urging, ghastly hands

in which nothing but
the ghost of love is held.

Damn it to hell.

NEIN

years nearly made for
a decade wherein

the word most germane
was *no*. You know?

Of course.
You. *Du*.

EPISTOLARY

(use as needed)

Those things I said, I *meant*.
But here is the letter I should have sent:

Dear BLANK.
I shall be brief, but frank,

terse if not curt, aloof, though unswerving—
what little we had amounted to nothing.

And yet I write you this missive, *as if*.
I sit on a sandbank as I scribe this,

for tonight the twilit beach is impossibly
gorgeous. No wind, no fog, no moody

sorts of weather. No the two of us together
like the last time, but *whatever*.

And on the verge of this horizon's indifference,
I watch as a ship slips into the distance.

And with it, my resistance to our over-ness.
Well, well. What a tideswell that idled between us.

The untidy-up-able mess
of your meanness, piles of petty treasons

birthed like broken promises, breech.
But I have not rung your cell phone now for weeks.

So our terminus no more consumes me.
And immutable dolors no more entomb me.

You see?
You have not ruined me.

And I was not mooning over you
when yesterday I fumbled through

slews of photo books and diaries, scrap
boxes and clipping files, tattering folders fat

with a miscellany of safeguarded ills,
brittle ordeals,

and souvenir glooms.
Reams

of curled-up edges and yellowing vellums.
Flotsam. Jetsam. *Comme*

ci, comme ça.
Que sera, sera.

No, I am not wistful as the mist is.
No, I do not brood as the brume does,

shrugging over your infinite ocean
like an omen

of momentous doom.
Soon, I'll disremember you,

forgetting every ebb and drag you tried.
We eddied. We surged, we broke. I waved *goodbye*.

I close this note
with *that alone*

in mind. And I seal this
epistle without a kiss,

without crying. I sign
this memo with a hieroglyphic

scratch. The door of us
slams shut

with a clobber and a thwack.
The sound of never turning back.

Like the drubbing of a hammer on the lid of a coffin.
How often do I think on you? *Not often.*

INSOMNIA IS LONELY

Though it needn't be.

It has me.

TIME

is a curve
with a caveat:

love can't stop it,
pause it, or posit

a theory of
recursive pasts.

Baby, ain't an entity
that lasts.

Carnations go mum,
tea turns cold,

all bright stars
become black holes

and even
paradise paroles

its tethers. Like
the man

who coos *always*.
But means *for never*.

TEAR

a tissue
ripped
to bits
is how
it ends

PRECIPICE

The border
of a thing.

Its edge
or hem.

The selvage,
the skirt,

a perimeter's
trim.

The blow
of daylight's

end and
nighttime's

beginning.
A fence

or a rim,
a margin,

a fringe.
And this:

the grim,
stingy

doorstep
where

the lapse
of passage

happens.
That slim

lip of land,
the liminal

verge
that slips

you past
your brink.

Where
and when

you
blink.

YES, BAUM

Oui, Tree.
I'm speaking

to yew. It's noon
and the mood

in which I'm currently
planted is as usual to me

as the spruce groves
in Norway—*sloe*

going, sloe gone. If yours
were the laurels

I'd longed for, *I lost.*
But ash to ash, as is

said. There is
no missed

tree here. In your
orchard I grew elder.

But the age
of us never became

me. Like an ersatz
ficus in a snazzed-up

parlor, I was out of your order,
your ardor, your arbor.

Hello,
Tallow.

It's juniper. It's June.
I lumber through

the clumsiest
of fuck yous. It isn't

a clear cut
retort.

Mullberry,
I've mulled

you over. Never con
a conifer.

Nothing lucky in our clovers.
True, we sat by the sea as lovers

but not all beeches
cease. We leave them,

right? Tamarak, oak,
take back your oaths.

let's settle it
with this cede-her sacrament:

neither for worse,
nor best, nor work,

nor forest, nor thicket,
nor thick of it.

Not for the aspen.
Not for the asp.

Neither the hemlock's
lockbox. Nor the pinebox

I'll bury my pining
in, once it dies.

Nor the bitter,
quinine orders

you barked.
Nor the cork

that held my heart's
hole closed when

even under pressure
of my palms

I couldn't stop the run
of resin

and I stayed trapped
for years in the lacquer

and the lack.
When is a walnut

a door? When the sign reads
entry.

Or, when there is
no exit.

I don't give
a fig

about your apples, Adam.
In Eden you gave me your name.

Linden? No.
It is no loan.

I earned it. I'll keep it.
I should.

Even if it burns
like poisonwood.

NIGHTWALK

The beekeeper's hut. The square, shared lots of the neighborhood gardens. A cemetery plot. A child's white coffin. You slip past them all with the old lamplit longings. But tonight the stars are skyless and your eyelid is scratched and you're crying. You pass a pack of sheepdogs. A barn. Barbed wire. The sole, open window of a small yellow house where a wife in a shoddy red robe has mantled her hair in a towel. (It's never. Or now.) And the city signs. And the welcome mats. The fact of a placard that spells out a speed bump. Apple trees ranked on the shoulder of the road. Do the sunflowers know they're eclipsed by the moon? You can't go home to a hell. The bench on the hill seems to sob. And church bells bang like pans and pots.

THE WISTFUL

A shirt is for unbuttoning.
A name is for forgetting.

Drunk is for getting.
And hillocks are for sitting on

and sighing, when, struck numb
by the sun's delinquent shining,

you resign to a strychnine indecisiveness
that's meant to discredit you.

You don't know what to do.
Or how. Or who.

Or if it even matters now, to boot.
And it suits you absolutely,

this languor, this drag.
Such as they were, your lusts

have been scissored in half.
And your heart.

That blood-blue slab
of vena cava and ventricle,

receptacle of kept loves,
villain, vile, and trivial—

it will take a final beating
then throw in its towel.

Then brake. Then coast.
Then slow to an almost

stock-still throb. Then—
if you're lucky—it stops.

WOULD-LAND

5 a.m. One-quarter past.
Distant chimes inform me this.

A bell peal knells the mist.
And sunlight's

not yet bludgeoning.
But some light gets blood going.

Last night it was snowing
and now

every path's a pall.
Though mine the only footfalls

at this hour of awe. Above
hangs a canopy of needle leaf.

Below, the season's
mean deceit—

that everything stays
white and clean.

It doesn't, of course,
but I wish it. My prayers

are green with this intent,
imploring winter wrens

to trill and begging scuttling bucks
come back.

There's something that I lack.
A wryneck

bullet-beaks a branch.
His woodworm didn't have a chance.

What I miss,
I've never had.

But I am not a ghost.
I am a guest.

And life is thirst,
at best.

So do not strike me, Heart.
I am, too, tinder.

I'm flammable
as birch bark, even damp.

Blue spruce, bee-eater—
be sweeter to me.

Let larksong shudder
to its January wheeze,

but gift these hands a happiness
just once.

It is half passed.
And I am cold.

Another peal has tolled.
I've told the sum of my appeals.

I need not watch for fox.
They do not congregate at dawn.

But I would,
were I one.

MARGINALIA

there is comfort in the company of ghosts

∞

all winter i walked in circles   were you there?
                                                              i think you were

∞

a bare, burned field?   *the plain, plane of pain*

∞

a mistake is a bed idea

∞

she lived a broad, domestic life, but felt foreign to herself

∞

what is your name

◐

never break bad news to boys on balconies and never
                                               underestimate july's late hate

◐

every crow's a counterfeit   i counted them all

◐

can a fire burn in the rain?

◐

i walked into your mouth as if it were an open door

◐

ugly as in

◐

look here, a button   and there, a knife
                                i know them   both

∞

never forget how fear you went

∞

there's hell in your hello

∞

he'd had it up to her

∞

never ask a ghost who he is
                            ask instead for what he wants

∞

mine: the face of someone who's mislaid a possession

∞

i sing on the cake

∞

i believe in love at first slight

∞

nothing spins in secret   also, nothing spins in   secret   also

∞

but how can i ever tryst you again?

∞

they were joined at the hope

∞

we were never clothes

∞

like waiting five years for a phone call

∞

the difference between a secret love and a secret, love

∞

you were a no-capped mountain
         it is no wonder

∞

sometimes a chair that isn't there, is

∞

your name is a joke my friends tell behind my back

∞

she was forgiven   she was forgotten

∞

i stood in the center of a sunflower field
         but radiated rain

∞

that can of worms? 　　　why, yes

　　　　　　　　　　　　　　　　let's open it

∞

to spread my legs like rumor: word-of-mouthly

∞

there's no place like him

∞

sadness, my soul companion

∞

she was made light of

∞

will I let the matter drop?
　　　　　absolutely not

　　　　　　　　　　i'm holding it to hurl at your head

∞

a bankbook to register the currencies of lovers

∞

i will not let you go until you bliss me

∞

every moon's a fool moon

∞

i took his sword for it

∞

his eye is on the sparrow but his hand is on the throttle

∞

she was sharp as attack

∞

that one great, white wail

∞

we can sordid out

∞

keys, please

there is something between us

∞

whatever turns you own

∞

just this				then one more hell

∞

you will never be free of everything you hate

heart, you're out for blood

ZÜRICHHORN

The night's blank vastness talks back.
You look to the lake. The blackness

plays tricks. Here the woman's sawn in
two. There she's seen in halves. Now

every man's a room, a groom, who heaves
his axe at her mouth. But dawn is a half-

dozen hours out and the clouds have
pooled to shut down sleep. Sheep cannot

be counted on now for the bellwether's
gone off his lead. You are alone more

often than not. A moonstone solitaire.
A ring. A saint or a seer of stockyard

ghosts. You wrack your red, wrong brain
and sieve for an answer that longs but

to grieve it. Look, look, look to the lake.
Then leave it.

ACKNOWLEDGMENTS AND NOTES

This book is dedicated to Jessica Piazza, who walked me through the shitstorm step by step.

Love and deep gratitude to all who helped me on my way to finishing this collection. A special shout-out is reserved for the NEA, without whose funding I could not have managed it at all.

I also want to thank my editor Adam Deutsch, who has one of the best damn ears in poetry, and also one of the best damn hearts. Mega props and love also to Christine Bryant and Max Xiantu—her for the whiz-bang copy edits and him for the kick-ass author image. Additionally, I give my profound and unending appreciation to Kathleen Anderson of Anderson Literary Management, who never fails to support, advise, and uphold me. Thank you, also, to Reb Livingston, Emily Atkinson, Lisa Billington, Wendy Duren, Tod Goldberg, Janna Lusk, Bree Rolfe, Cheryl Schneider, Jay Schulz, my UCR colleagues, my students, and all whom I love, who have both endured and encouraged me over the last years. You're the best. All y'all. And finally to my husband, Alvin Peng, I say this: you are everything; we are forever.

Many, many magical thanks to the journals in which these poems first appeared in either early or final form:

42 Poems: "Epistolary," *Alaska Quarterly Review:* "Two Story," *The American Poetry Journal:* "Outside," *The Arkansas International:* "Yes, Baum," *The Book of Scented Things:* "Miserere Mei," *Cellpoems:* "Insomnia is Lonely," *The Christian Century:* "Im Friedhof," *Goliad Review:* "Illusion," "To Vanish," "The Hours," *Gulf Coast:* "Stays," *Image:* "Apologia," *Moira:* "Civil Twilight," "Nightwalk," *No Tell Motel:* "She Was Driven By a Thousand Desires, a Few of Them Decent," "Passage" (as "Im Aegert"), "Rapsfeld," "everywhere a magpie," "What a dream I had," "Zürichhorn," *Oranges and Sardines:* "You Cannot Rescue a Woman From Herself"

Poetry: "Non Redibimus," "Easter," "4:13 a.m.," "What Isn't Mine" "Poem," "Precipice," "Would- Land," "Parting Song," "She Spent a Year Hallucinating Birds," *Read America(s):* "I Am Most Myself," *Smartish Pace:* "Zürich Hauptbahnhof," *The Sunday Rumpus:* "The Run-Down," "Time"

"Greifensee" and "The Wistful" first appeared in the appendix to the paperback version of my novel *Hausfrau*.

"Apologia" and "Stays" were included in the 2010 and 2011 editions of the *Best American Poetry* anthologies, respectively.

Zürich Hauptbahnhof is the city's main train station.

Rapsfeld translates to "field of rapeseed."

The Greifensee is the second largest lake in Canton Zürich, and it's spooky on grey days.

Miserere Mei is Latin for "Have mercy on me."

Im Friedhof translates to "in the cemetery."

Civil twilight refers to the approximate limit at which solar illumination is sufficient, under clear weather conditions, for terrestrial objects to be clearly distinguished.

"Nightwalk" is for Jennifer Carrera Bognar.

Marginalia is just that: notes and one-line poems.

Zürichhorn is a river delta on Lake Zürich's eastern shore in the lower basin of the lake.

Jill Alexander Essbaum is the award-winning author of several collections of poetry including *Heaven, Harlot, Necropolis,* and the single-poem chapbook *The Devastation*. Her first novel, *Hausfrau,* debuted on the *New York Times* Bestseller List and has been translated into 26 languages. Her work has appeared in dozens of journals including *Poetry, The Christian Century, Image,* and *The Rumpus,* as well as multiple *Best American Poetry* anthologies. A two-time NEA fellow, Jill is a core faculty member in The Low Residency MFA Program at University of California-Palm Desert. She lives in Austin, Texas.

www.ingramcontent.com/pod-product-compliance
Lightning Source LLC
Chambersburg PA
CBHW030345100526
44592CB00010B/832